A Wisley Handbook

Bedding
Plants

GRAHAM RICE

Cassell

The Royal Horticultural Society

THE ROYAL HORTICULTURAL SOCIETY

Cassell Educational Limited
Villiers House, 41/47 Strand
London WC2N 5JE
for the Royal Horticultural Society

First published 1993

British Library Cataloguing in Publication Data
A catalogue record for this book is available from
the British Library

ISBN 0-304-32025-0

Photographs by Roger Hyam (pp. 26, 36); Andrew Lawson (p. 61);
Photos Horticultural (pp. 4, 17, 18, 22, 42, 44, 46, 50, 53); Graham Rice
(pp. 6, 28, 30, 34, 40, 41, 62) and Harry Smith Collection (pp. 11, 15, 21,
31, 38, 43, 49, 54, 56, 59, 60)

Line drawings by Mike Shoebridge

Typeset by Litho Link Limited, Welshpool, Powys

Printed in Hong Kong by Wing King Tong Co. Ltd

Cover: *Verbena* 'Sissinghurst' and *Felicia amelloides* 'Santa
Anita Variegated' are both tender perennials and superb
for bedding out.
Back cover: Grandiflora petunias have large flowers.
   Photographs by Andrew Lawson
p1: *Tagetes* 'Tangerine Gem' is a mass of flowers all
summer long, providing plants are deadheaded
regularly.
   Photograph by Photos Horticultural

Contents

Introduction

Bedding plants have two impressive features in their favour. First of all they are among the most colourful of all plants, flowering for an exceptionally long period compared with most shrubs and perennials, and are available in almost any shade and colour imaginable. Secondly, they are extremely easy to grow and many respond heroically to the minimum of care and attention. Yet, despite these overwhelming arguments, many gardeners are wary of bedding plants because of the need to replace them regularly.

Bedding plants are, by definition, temporary in nature, for they are essentially raised and grown in one place, then planted out for a single season display in another. There was a time when plants were changed three or four times a year; even perennials such as lupins and Michaelmas daisies were planted out for a limited period and removed after flowering. These days we normally make only two changes a year: the summer flowering plants are set out in late spring or early summer and replaced in the autumn by plants that will stand through the winter to give spring colour.

Traditional bedding plants – bright red salvias and 'geraniums', white alyssum and blue lobelia – although still widely used, in recent years have been joined by a new range of plants. These are the tender perennials, an essential part of any hanging basket or pot planting. Many are covered with showy flowers throughout the summer, a prime requisite for any bedding plant. Others have attractive foliage, and a particularly useful group naturally trail over the edge of containers and weave schemes together.

Much advice on bedding plants has been based on the practices of commercial nurseries and parks departments But large-scale techniques are not always suitable for home gardeners with more limited facilities. Bedding plants can be bought ready-raised from garden centres, but many can be raised successfully at home with little in the way of specialist equipment, either from seed or from cuttings. Some need to be started in fairly high temperatures but, with one of the range of heated propagators now available, even this is not a problem.

Annual summer bedding with heliotropium, silver-foliaged cineraria and white alyssum

Summer Plants

Summer bedding plants are generally frost tender and are grown to planting size under protection before being bedded out after the last frost, generally in late May or early June. Even hardy species which are to be bedded out for the summer are raised in this way. They fall into two main categories: those raised afresh from seed each year and those overwintered as plants in frost-free conditions and propagated by cuttings.

SUMMER BEDDING FROM SEED

The majority of summer bedding plants are raised from seed early in the year. They may be half hardy annuals such as zinnias, hardy annuals such as alyssum or tender perennials such as zonal pelargoniums, which are treated as half hardy annuals. All are raised by sowing seed in warmth in early spring, growing on and then hardening off before planting out in beds and borders.

Many bedding plants can be raised on a windowsill but a greenhouse and heated propagator will give them the best start.

Greenhouse

Few gardeners erect a greenhouse specifically for the raising of bedding plants; an existing greenhouse will usually be used. However, the one feature of a new greenhouse that would be a great advantage to the bedding plant raiser is a built-in partition dividing off a small area, perhaps one third of a 12 ft × 8 ft (4 × 2.5 m) greenhouse. Some greenhouse manufacturers can supply a partition to fit into an existing structure but if this is not possible a carefully fitted rigid polythene sheet will do the job.

This small, partitioned area can be heated in early spring when heating is at its most expensive, without the need to waste energy on heating the whole greenhouse. A propagator can be installed in this area and, since it is already in a slightly heated environment, will itself use less energy. A thermostatically controlled heated mat could also be used on the staging in this area.

Argyranthemum 'Jamaica Primrose', *Salvia farinacea* 'Victoria' and *Helichrysum petiolare* 'Limelight'

Alongside the greenhouse, a cold frame is invaluable, especially in those last frosty nights of spring when so many plants demand protection and facilities become very congested. This can be an off-the-shelf aluminium structure or, better still, a home-made frame constructed of insulating blocks, old railway sleepers or tongue-and-grooved boards which can be built as large as (or preferably larger) than needed, and topped with glass- or polythene-glazed lights.

Windowsill

Plants raised on windowsills indoors will not usually match the quality of those raised in better conditions in the greenhouse. However, once planted out they have a habit of catching up as summer growth develops. If you can tolerate propagators and pots scattered around the house, then take advantage of the differing light conditions afforded by windows of different aspects and the varying temperatures available in different rooms in the house. By moving seedlings and young plants from one place to another as they grow, and as the season warms, it is possible to minimize the effects of the low, one-sided lighting and of the dry atmosphere.

Propagator and heated mat

An electrically heated propagator is the most important item of your seed-raising equipment and it should incorporate an adjustable thermostat so that the temperature can be set accurately. Many models are available, from one-seed-tray size to larger models taking half a dozen trays or as many as 60 small pots. If you grow many plants and work on a large scale, you could build your own propagating frame on the greenhouse bench, using timber sides and base, soil-warming cables with a thermostat, plus a glass- or polythene-glazed lid. Although individual seeds vary in their requirements, a temperature of 65-70°F (18-21°C) suits most.

For windowsill seed raising, long, narrow propagators specially designed to fit on a sill are available. In addition to a heated model a couple of unheated propagators are also valuable to provide an intermediate stage between the cosy conditions in the heated propagator and the harsher world outside.

In the greenhouse, intermediate conditions are also necessary and may be provided in a number of ways. The greenhouse itself can be heated slightly, part of the greenhouse can be partitioned off and only this area heated, or a larger frame within the greenhouse can be built and maintained at an intermediate temperature. In all these cases a growing temperature of 45°F (7°C) represents the best compromise between ideal growing conditions and energy conservation. A good alternative is to install a heated mat which keeps the roots of the plants at a relatively high temperature, about 60°F (15°C), and which allows the air temperature to be kept just frost-free. This will give a net saving in energy and also encourage short bushy growth.

Pots and trays
For most gardeners it is extremely wasteful to sow seed in seed trays unless very large numbers of plants are needed. Do you really want to raise 500 antirrhinums? Plastic pots 3 in. (8 cm) or 4 in. (10 cm) across, preferably square ones, will enable you to raise all you need while being as economical of space as possible; if you do need an especially large number of some plants, sow in two or three pots. For the later stages of growth I also prefer square pots, as these not only provide the flexibility to fill every inch of space without the awkward wasteful gaps sometimes left by the seed trays, but offer individual plants more root room, so that they suffer less disturbance when planted out. I tend to grow small quantities of a large range of plants, but if you prefer to raise large numbers of relatively few genera, pricking out into trays is probably more sensible.

If you use trays, the extra root room provided by deep trays is invaluable; the plants will be of better quality, while the extra

Left to right: cellular polystyrene tray; moulded plastic seed tray; standard tray with interlocking dividers

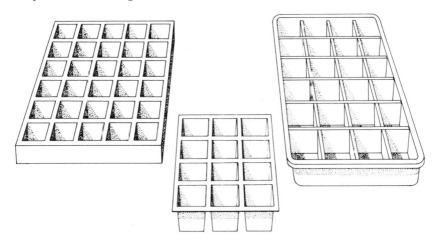

compost gives them a larger water reserve, invaluable if you go away for the weekend and the weather turns hot. Although such trays are more expensive, they are usually made of stouter materials, so last longer.

Recently, I have found propagating trays a very useful alternative. These plastic trays are divided into small cells, each of which accommodates one young plant. Seed is sown individually or in pinches in the small-sized cells and then each plug of compost with its germinated seedlings is moved to a larger cell or pot with no root disturbance. This minimizes root damage and prevents setbacks in growth.

Compost
Loam-based, peat-based and coir-based composts can all be used to raise bedding plants but each has its own special requirements. Try to avoid using more than one type at a time as this makes it more difficult to give each the care it needs. I avoid loam-based composts for bedding plants as the quality is very unpredictable, and a poor loam-based compost is difficult to improve. Peat-based composts are less variable and also lighter in weight, and bedding plants grow well in them. Coir composts and other peat substitutes are relatively new and vary noticeably from brand to brand. My advice is to stick to one brand and get used to it. The one thing all coir composts seem to have in common is that the surface dries out quickly while underneath the compost remains moist, so careful watering is necessary.

SOWING TECHNIQUES

Tip out some seed compost from its bag on to your potting bench (or polythene-covered kitchen table!), fluff it up and make sure it is moist but not soggy. Ensure that the pots for seed sowing are clean and gather together everything else you will need: clingfilm or glass, plus newspaper for covering seed pots, a watering can with a fine rose, labels and marker pen, and a presser.

If you are sowing more than just one or two genera, start by filling pots about half a dozen at a time. Fill each pot loosely to the brim, wipe off the surplus level with the rim of the pot then tap the pot on the bench to settle the compost; finally, firm very gently to level the surface, using a home-made presser. A presser can be made from a round of plywood or anything about the right size to fit inside a 3 in. (8 cm) pot with angular rather than rounded edges; a plastic beaker is sometimes suitable. The surface of the

Cineraria 'Silver Dust' (see p.21) and fibrous-rooted begonias can both be raised from seed, although the seed of the begonias is very fine

compost should be about ¼ in (6 mm) below the rim of the pot. Now open your first seed packet, remove the smaller inner foil packet inside, cut the top off with scissors and inspect the contents.

Consider now how many plants you need to grow and decide whether to sow all the seed or just some of it, whether it will all go in one seed pot or whether you need another. It is difficult to advise on exactly how much seed to sow in each pot as some seeds are so much bigger than others. But bear in mind that although a pot will take more begonia seedlings than zinnia seeds, the temptation to fill a pot with large numbers of tiny begonias or lobelias should be resisted.

The seed must be sown thinly and evenly over the surface of the compost. For all but the largest seed I find that the best method is as follows. Having cut the top off the inner packet, make a crease half-way along one of the cut edges. Hold the packet between the thumb and middle finger, tip the packet slightly so that the seed tends to run into the crease, then tap the edge of the packet with index finger to encourage the seed to roll off the edge and on to the compost. This way you can see exactly how much seed is falling on to the compost, and by moving the packet back and forth as the seed falls, the surface can be covered evenly.

Larger seeds such as marigolds and dahlias need less careful sowing and can be redistributed over the surface of the compost after sowing by moving them with the point of a pencil. Very small seeds like those of lobelias, petunias and begonias can be tricky, but the method I have described will distribute the seed evenly, although this is less easy if your eyesight is poor. The old trick of adding a small amount of very dry silver sand to the seed, mixing thoroughly and sowing the highly visible mixture, works well. Large seeds can be sown in twos in individual pots, thinned to one as they develop and then potted on before planting out.

After sowing, most seed needs a covering of compost, although plants with small seeds like begonias and petunias can simply be pressed gently into the surface of the compost. Over the years I have found that this gentle pressing is very useful, reducing the amount of fine compost that needs sifting over the seed to a covering as deep as the seed itself. Some gardeners use an old kitchen sieve for this purpose but I find this is too fine and use a home-made sieve made by tacking a square of greenhouse shade netting to a light wooden frame. Vermiculite can also be used as a seed covering but is less easy to manage than compost. Immediately after sowing, write the label giving the name, source of seed and date of sowing.

AFTER SOWING

Once a few pots have been sown, they need watering. I prefer to water gently with a fine rose on a watering can, tipping the can to get the water flowing before moving the spray over the pots, then moving it away before stopping – this avoids huge drips disturbing the seeds. Some gardeners prefer to stand their seed pots in a bowl of water so that water is soaked up from below until the surface darkens; but when the pots are removed, peat-based composts tend to shrink away from the sides of the pots. In either case it pays to add a copper fungicide to the water to help prevent damping off.

When surplus water has drained away, the pots can go in the propagator. Most seeds do not need any more darkness to encourage germination than is provided by their covering of compost, and are covered with paper (brown paper or old newspaper will suffice) simply to prevent them becoming too hot.

If your germinated seeds are removed from the propagator as soon as they sprout, the whole propagator can be covered with paper. If your facilities are restricted, the seed pots must be covered individually.

The pots will need a clear moisture-retentive covering under the paper. If large seed trays have been used, a rectangle of glass and a piece of paper can cover each tray. On a small scale, this is more difficult. Fine, uncovered seed is in particular danger of drying out and here a piece of clingfilm stretched over the pot is useful. Some gardeners use rounds of glass or rigid plastic, some use larger sheets of glass to cover a number of pots. I find that for most seeds, if the lid is on the propagator, it is covered with paper to exclude sun and is not placed in a sunny spot, then no additional moisture-retentive covering is required, although careful misting or gentle watering may sometimes be necessary.

Once in the propagator, seeds should be checked twice a day as some, like marigolds and dahlias, germinate very quickly. As soon as they appear, any paper covering should be removed and then glass or clingfilm removed a day or two later. At this stage the pots are best moved to a slightly cooler temperature where the seedlings can grow on until the seed leaves have expanded. Watering should be checked regularly, and a copper fungicide added to the water as a precaution against damping off.

PRICKING OUT

The usual suggestion is to prick out the seedlings 'when they are large enough to handle'. Generally, this is good advice although certain small seedlings like lobelias will be quite well developed by this stage. For most plants the 'large enough to handle' stage is reached when the first pair of leaves, the seed leaves, are well developed. The later you leave it after this stage, the more root damage will affect their later growth.

Water the seed pot well with fungicide a few hours beforehand and moisten your potting compost. The usual advice is to use the same type of compost for pricking out as for seed sowing but if the seedlings are small this is of little importance. Make sure that your pots or boxes are clean and likewise your dibber and presser.

Fill the pots in the same way as the seed pots, although there is no need to firm with a presser. Use the dibber or an old dinner fork to remove some seedlings from the seed pot or alternatively tip the entire contents carefully on the bench. Make a hole with the dibber in the centre of the pot deep and wide enough to take the full length of root without breaking it. Carefully extract a single seedling, place it in position with its seed leaves just above soil level, and tap the pot sharply on the bench to settle the soil around the roots. Firming the seedling in place with the dibber or the fingers is often recommended but with peat-based compost this can lead to over-firming. A few brisk taps, followed by watering, settles the compost well around the roots without compacting it too much. Over-firmed compost leading to waterlogging and rot is the main cause of failures.

Trays for pricking out are filled in a similar way although it pays to half-fill the tray and press the compost carefully into the corners and along the edges before topping up and striking off the surplus. On this larger scale the use of a purpose-made presser is advisable as it is more difficult to settle a trayful of compost by tapping; but only gentle firming is required.

The number of seedlings you prick out into each tray depends on the size of the tray and the vigour of the plant. As a rule, 24 would be more appropriate in a standard seed tray. Tomato boxes are larger and deeper, so can take more.

Start by pricking out a seedling into each of three corners, then mark the central point along a short and a long side with the dibber; if an odd number of seedlings is to go along the side, set one seedling in the middle and lay others equally spaced along the two halves to give you the required number. If an even number are to go in, place a seedling on either side of your mark and then divide up the two sides in the same way. Make holes with the dibber and plant the seedlings as before. This leaves you with two rows of seedlings along adjacent sides to serve as a guide for the positioning of the rest of the seedlings. Now prick out the rest of seedlings, filling each short row steadily across the tray. Tap the box and water the seedlings in well with a copper fungicide.

CARE TO PLANTING TIME

After pricking out, the pots or boxes do not require as high a temperature as was needed for seed germination; nevertheless, a relatively high temperature, even for just a few days, helps root growth to start promptly. I stand my pricked-out seedlings on a heated mat giving a root temperature of 60°F (15°C), with a minimum air temperature of 45°F (7°C). In fact, with care in watering and attention to good ventilation and disease prevention, night air temperatures of just above freezing will still produce good plants.

14

Cosmos 'Sonata White' (see p.21) with pelargoniums and marigolds planted out in blocks in a special display bed

I find that the stage when the seedlings are moved off the mat and on to the open bench is generally governed not so much by choosing the optimum stage of growth, but by the need to find space on the mat for the next batch. Most gardeners are limited for greenhouse space and even the addition of high level shelves and the utilization of the space below the benches may not provide enough scope for moving the plants to the next stage at the very best moment. Fortunately, bedding plants are tough and adaptable and can usually cope with less than perfect conditions as long as growing techniques are adapted accordingly.

Some plants like antirrhinums, calceolarias, gazanias and other almost-hardy plants are best grown as cool as possible to encourage branching and prevent lanky growth. They will do best if kept just frost free.

For most people, the space problem is at its most acute at the stage when the plants are developing well and in need of spacing out, whilst still requiring protection from the last spring frosts. This is the hardening-off stage when plants are acclimatized to the outside world after being cosseted in artificially warm conditions for the first months of their life.

For windowsill gardeners, the sill of an unheated spare room in the house may be a convenient spot for a period, followed perhaps by a windowsill in the garage. There may be space for a small cold frame in the garden for the final stage or plants can be moved outside during the day and moved back to the garage when frost threatens; or they could be left in a sheltered porch.

For gardeners with more facilities, a cold frame is the answer, and the bigger the better, hence the earlier suggestion of a home-made frame. Some cold frames are so expensive that a cheap aluminium greenhouse seems a better buy. But whether you use a cold frame or cold greenhouse for hardening off, the idea is to expose the young plants increasingly to outside conditions by reducing their protection. This is done by opening vents or removing frame lights on blue-sky days, then on chillier days, while closing them at night when frost threatens or in spells of cold wind or heavy rain. For the last couple of weeks before planting, the plants should have the maximum possible exposure to the weather.

During this period the young plants should never be allowed to dry out and should be fed every 10-14 days, depending on the weather, with a general purpose liquid fertilizer. They should also be protected from slugs and inspected regularly for other pests and diseases. Most modern cultivars are bred to branch well from low down to create a bushy plant without the need for pinching out, but older kinds may need their tips pinched out and this should be done when the plants are relatively small. In general, I am against routine pinching, and prefer to rely on giving the individual plants sufficient space for their natural branching to develop.

PLANTING OUT

Although most bedding plants are generally fairly tough and adaptable, good soil preparation pays off. In soil of good fertility, loosening the soil with a border fork to the full depth of the tines and removing weeds is often enough. The soil should then be trodden well and a dressing of 2-4 oz (55-110 g) per square yard or metre of a general fertilizer such as blood, fish and bone or Growmore raked in before planting. When bedding plants are grown on their own in beds reserved for temporary displays, annual additions of organic matter, such as rotted manure or garden compost, are invaluable. Whether you dig this in before planting the summer bedding, or in the autumn before planting spring bedding, will depend on your soil: apply it in autumn to

A window box full of summer bedding – petunias, lobelia, pelargoniums –
none tall enough to darken the room

heavy clay soils and in spring to lighter sandy soils.

When bedding plants are set in small groups in mixed borders,
the degree of preparation required for individual planting sites
will depend on the overall fertility of the soil. If the border has
recently been replanted and plenty of organic matter dug in, a
sprinkling of 2 oz (55 g) fertilizer per square yard or metre will
suffice. If it is some years since this was done, then forking in
well-rotted compost or one of the peat substitutes followed by
fertilizer at double the rate may be more appropriate. Where
individual plants are set out in a mixed border, I use a planting
mix made up of a two-gallon bucket of old potting or seed compost
mixed with 2 oz (55 g) of fertilizer, and this is worked into the soil
immediately before planting.

Plants must be moist when planted and I like to give them a
final liquid feed a few hours beforehand. Plants from pots are
planted with a trowel, those from trays are best removed in one
block and then separated by pulling them apart. After planting
and firming in well, water them again individually with liquid
feed to ensure that there are readily available nutrients for the new
roots to utilize.

A to Z of Plants
Raised from Seed

This descriptive list of the most important seed-raised bedding plants is intended to give an idea of the impressive range now available, to select especially good cultivars from the thousands on offer and to give advice on any special requirements they may have. Seed packets now give increasingly comprehensive instructions and should be consulted before sowing.

Ageratum Clusters of fluffy flowers in various blues, pinks and white. Although blue ageratums reproduce badly in pictures in seed catalogues, in general they make better plants than those with pink flowers, and white flowers tend to brown as they die. Good smaller cultivars for edging and the front of the border are the spreading 'Blue Swords', 8 in. (20 cm), mid blue, the more compact and purplish 'North Sea', 8 in. (20 cm), and the larger-leaved, azure 'Blue Mink', 9 in. (23 cm). 'Southern Cross', 10 in. (25 cm), is a lovely blue and white bicolour while 'Pinky', 8 in. (20 cm), and 'Summer Snow', 8 in. (20 cm), give pink and white. Tall types for the back of the border and for cutting include 'Blue Horizon', 2 ft (60 cm), and the white 'Highness', 2 ft (60 cm).

Do not cover the seed, simply press it into the compost and prick out into pots if possible

Alyssum (*Lobularia maritima*) Flat carpeting plants in white, various pinks, lilacs and purples; the darker colours are generally less vigorous than the white. 'Snow Crystals', 4 in (10 cm), is a neat, large-flowered, well-scented white while 'Carpet of Snow', 4 in. (10 cm), spreads to 15 in. (38 cm). 'Rosie O'Day' is a good pink, 'Wonderland' the best purple, and 'Creamery' a new pale cream shade. Pastel Carpet and Morning Mist are good mixtures.

Although alyssum can be grown as a hardy annual it is often raised as a bedding plant. Prick out seedlings of mixtures in threes to get the best tapestry effect. Do not overwater in boxes and watch for grey mould (*Botrytis*).

Antirrhinum Commonly known as snapdragon, these are now

Impatiens (see p.23) are ideal plants for shady places. This New Guinea hybrid has strongly variegated foliage available in a wide range of sizes and colours. Unfortunately rust is a problem and no varieties are completely resistant. The best mixtures with the usual, two-lipped flowers include Floral Carpet and Tahiti, 8-10 in. (20-25 cm), Coronette, Monarch and Sonnet, 15-18 in. (38-45 cm), and Giant Forerunner, 3 ft (1 m). Doubles include Sweetheart, 12 in. (30 cm) and Madame Butterfly, 2½ ft (75 cm), open-throated types include Little Darling, 12 in. (30 cm) (see p. 61) and Trumpet Serenade, 18 in. (45 cm). Brighton Rock, 18 in. (45 cm), is the first of the reintroduced Victorian striped antirrhinums. Some of the finest antirrhinums are single colours in the medium height range and these include 'Black Prince' with bronze leaves and deep purple flowers, 'Lavender Monarch', and 'Princess Purple and White', a lovely bicolour.

Grow cool to promote branching and beware of damping off. Spray all cultivars regularly, even those said to be rust resistant, with propiconazole. Cut back plants after flowering and water well to promote a second flush of flowers.

Aster (*Callistephus chinensis*) Relatively late-flowering plants once used mainly for cutting; dwarfer forms are now available for bedding. Wilt is an incurable soil disease which attacks asters grown in the same soil for too long; and none are completely resistant. A wide variety of flower forms is available including singles, chrysanthemum-flowered, ostrich-feathered, quilled, incurved, pompon and crested. Mixtures for edging and the front of the border include the incurved Milady, 10 in. (25 cm), the lovely quilled Teisa Stars, 10 in. (25 cm), and the small ostrich-feathered Comet, 8 in. (20 cm). Good taller mixtures include the single Andrella, 2½ ft (75 cm), Pompon, 18 in. (45 cm), which includes bicolours and tricolours, the chrysanthemum-flowered Riviera, 2 ft (60 cm), and the incurved Duchess, 2 ft (60 cm).

Beware of damping off, prick out taller types into individual pots if possible. To obtain a reasonable display on wilt-infected soil, pot on plants into 5 in. (13 cm) pots to give them a reservoir of uninfected soil. Remember that asters start into flower later than most bedders, so site them accordingly.

Begonia Begonias for bedding fall into two groups. Large-flowered tuberous-rooted begonias have flamboyant double flowers in a wide range of colours while small-flowered, fibrous-rooted begonias have single flowers in a more restricted range. Seed of tuberous begonias is more expensive so they are often preferred for containers and they usually come only in mixtures.

The well-known tuberous Non Stop, 9 in. (23 cm), comes in ten colours and now has a bronze-leaved cousin, Non Stop Ornament.

Aster Pompon (see opposite) is one of the taller growing selections suitable for planting in a mixed border

Musical, 9 in. (23 cm), in four colours, has a more trailing habit while the semi-double Chanson in five shades is a genuine trailer. 'Pin-Up', 9 in. (23 cm) (see p. 22), is a single white with a pink picotee. Fibrous-rooted begonias come in green-leaved and bronze-leaved types, with flowers in the red/pink/white range; most are compact and bushy although a few have a trailing habit. Again most come as mixtures and for mixes including those with green and bronzed leaves try Lucia, 8 in. (20 cm), (Devon Gems and New Generation are similar), or the larger-flowered Party Fun, 12 in. (30 cm). Olympia, 8 in. (20 cm), is a good green-leaved mix, Cocktail, 8 in. (20 cm) is a good bronze-leaved mix. Individual colours worth considering include 'Coco Ducolor', 12 in. (30 cm), with bronze leaves and pink-edged white flowers, 'Danica Red', 10 in. (25 cm), with bronze leaves and scarlet flowers and the trailing green-leaved 'Pink Avalanche'.

Leave uncovered after sowing but keep humidity high by covering with clingfilm, water from below and keep the temperature at 70°F (21°C) or above if possible. Beware of damping off. Plant in rich soil. The fibrous types in particular will take partial shade.

Cineraria (*Senecio bicolor* subsp. *cineraria*) Silver-leaved plants for foliage borders or among flowering plants; a good foil for many other plants and may overwinter in mild seasons. 'Silver Dust', 9 in. (23 cm) (see p. 11), has deeply cut foliage while 'Cirrus', 12 in. (30cm), is an oak-leaved type with lobed leaves. Easy to raise.

'Pin-Up' is a showy tuberous-rooted begonia with an upright growth habit
(see p.20)

Cosmos Vigorous plants with attractive finely cut foliage and large, single daisy flowers all summer. All are good in bedding and for cutting. The mixtures come in various reds, pinks and white with some bicolours. Sensation, 3-4 ft (1-1.2 m), is the standard mixture while Sonata, 2 ft (60 cm), is the best dwarf type. The lovely Sea Shells, 3 ft (1 m), has the petals rolled into fluted tubes. Among the single colours, 'Sonata White', 18 in. (45 cm) (see p. 15) and 'Purity', 3-4 ft (1-1.2 m), both white, are stunning, as is the pink-eyed white 'Daydream', 3-4 ft (1-1.2 m).

Easy to raise, cosmos are vigorous and are best pricked out into individual pots. In the garden they make bushy plants and may need support in windy areas. Dead head or cut for the house regularly. Can be sown *in situ* in May.

Dahlia It is only worth raising dwarfer dahlias from seed; the taller large-flowered dahlias are better grown from tubers. Dahlias will often be in flower when planted and then continue until the frosts. Usually available only in mixtures, a few single colours are now being listed. Coltness Hybrids, 18 in. (45 cm), are single flowered in a wide range of shades, Unwins Dwarf Hybrids, 2 ft (60 cm) is a fine semi-double mix and Dandy, 2ft (60 cm), has a collar of quilled petals around the eye; Figaro, 12 in. (30 cm), is the best dwarf. Redskin, 18 in. (45 cm), and Diablo, 12 in. (30 cm), are bronze-leaved mixtures, although their flowers tend to be rather watery in colour.

Easy to raise and will germinate well at 60°F (15°C), then best pricked out into individual pots when they can be grown on very cool. Beware of aphids. Lift any plants you especially like and store the tubers.

Dianthus The best bedding dianthus are colourful and long flowering but some are far too dumpy and are better as pot plants. They come in carnation types and those which are more like single pinks. Of the carnation types Knight, 12 in. (30 cm), is a good dwarf mixture but few colours are scented, the powerfully fragrant Giant Chabaud Mixed, 2 ft (60 cm), is wonderful in a large bed while 'Scarlet Luminette', 2ft. (60 cm), is a sparkling colour for borders or cutting. Ideal, 12 in. (30 cm), Telstar, 9 in. (23 cm), and Princess, 9 in. (23 cm), are all fine mixtures with good colours while as individual shades try the blood-red 'Telstar Crimson', 9 in. (23 cm), 'Snow Fire', 9 in. (23 cm), in white with a scarlet eye, and 'Colour Magician', 9 in. (23 cm), which opens white and fades to deep pink.

Best sown in a seed compost rather than multi-purpose compost as dianthus dislike high nutrient levels. Grow cool to encourage bushiness and plant out in full sun or partial shade. Prolonged drought may curtail flowering. All, in fact, are perennials and may overwinter in well-drained conditions.

Gazania Flamboyant low-growing plants with daisy flowers in many sunny shades, some also have silvery foliage. The flowers stay closed on cool, dull days but are stunning in sunnier conditions. The dwarf Mini-Star, 8 in. (20 cm), has a wide range of colours and the white and yellow may be available separately. Talent, 8 in. (20 cm), is similar but has grey foliage while Sundance, 12 in. (30 cm), has much larger flowers at 4 in. (10 cm) across, many of them striped, and is good for cutting.

Easy to raise and can be grown cool after pricking out, gazanias are also hardier than most bedders so can be planted out a little earlier. Always plant in full sun; shelter is an advantage.

Geranium see **Pelargonium**

Impatiens The popular busy lizzies are adaptable plants in an impressive range of shades and a vast number of cultivars. Impatiens are the best bedders for shady positions but may flower poorly in hot, dry conditions. Eventual height depends greatly on growing conditions, shade and moisture producing the tallest plants.

The best mixtures, in ascending order of eventual plant height, are Super Elfin, 6-8 in. (15-20 cm), Accent, Expo, Tempo and Blitz, 12-15 in. (30-38 cm). Super Elfin has the biggest colour range, Blitz has the largest flowers. Super Elfin Pearl, 6-8 in. (15-20 cm), is a stunning pastel mixture, Eye Eye, 8 in. (20 cm), is a lovely mixture of eyed cultivars, and Starbright, 8 in. (20 cm), is a mixture of colours with white stars. Rosette will give a good proportion of doubles. Spectra is a large-flowered mixture of New Guinea hybrids, many with variegated foliage (see p. 18). Separate colours are available from many of these mixtures and I would recommend the unique 'Tempo Burgundy', the picotee 'Super Elfin Swirl', the stunning 'Expo White' and the exceptionally floriferous 'Salmon Profusion', 9 in. (23 cm).

Sow in a well-drained seed compost, press the seed into the surface and do not cover; keep humid. Water with tepid water and feed sparingly. Prick out before true leaves develop, reduce temperatures gradually for growing on and harden off gently. Busy Lizzies react poorly to sudden changes of conditions.

Lobelia The bush and trailing types are our most popular blue-flowered bedders but are now available in an increasing variety of other shades. Expect a few blues amongst the whites. Bush types reach about 6 in. (15 cm); 'Crystal Palace' is the darkest with slightly bronzed foliage, 'Mrs Clibran' is dark with a white eye, 'Cambridge Blue' is paler. There is also 'Rosamund' in purplish red and 'White Lady'. Many mixtures are available but Kaleidoscope has the best range. Among trailers the white-eyed 'Sapphire' is the darkest blue while 'Light Blue Fountain' is sky blue; there are also the more or less self explanatory 'Ruby Cascade', 'Lilac Fountain' and 'Rose Fountain'. In mixtures Fountain is especially floriferous and not too straggly while giving the most diverse range of colours.

Surface sow thinly and cover with clingfilm to keep moist. Prick out in small patches of seedlings and grow cool once established to improve bushiness. Beware of damping off.

Marigold There are three kinds of marigolds: French, African and hybrids between the two. The French are generally smaller in habit and flower size, have single or double flowers and are available in yellows, golds, oranges, chestnut and mahogany shades and in various combinations. The Africans have dense, fully double flowers and are medium or tall with flowers in a narrower yellow/gold/orange range. The Afro-French hybrids tend to be medium in height, single or double, and mainly in the African colours.

The best single-flowered French marigolds are the Mischief, 12 in. (30 cm), series, available as a mixture and single colours, while for something shorter try Espagna, 8-10 in. (20-25 cm). 'Red

Marietta', 8 in. (20 cm), in mahogany-red edged in orange is one of a number of colours available separately. In doubles good mixtures are Boy-O-Boy, 6 in. (15 cm), and Sophia, 10 in. (25 cm), with the brilliant coloured 'Yellow Jacket', 8 in. (20 cm), and the unique 'Safari Tangerine', 9 in. (23 cm), both good separates. In recent years African marigolds have become shorter and larger flowered, but are still only available in yellow, gold and orange. Inca, Perfection and Discovery are all good dwarf, large-flowered mixtures with some colours available individually. They can all look rather squashed and dumpy and may suffer in wet weather although they are good in containers. Gay Ladies, 15 in. (38 cm), and Crackerjack, 3 ft (1 m), suffer less in bad weather and look better in the garden. The primrose-yellow 'Doubloon', 2½ ft (75 cm), is a good separate. Afro-French marigolds set no seed and so are very prolific and need no dead heading. Zenith, 10 in. (25 cm), is a wonderful double-flowered mix as is the slightly taller Solar, 14 in. (35 cm), with the mahogany 'Seven Star Red', 12 in. (30 cm), an outstanding separate colour. 'Susie Wong', 12 in. (30 cm), is a good lemony single.

All marigolds have large seeds which are easy to sow and they grow quickly so can be sown late to minimize on heat. The Africans are best pricked out into individual pots and planted before they start to flower. Plant all marigolds in full sun and dead head regularly to prolong flowering, this also improves the appearance of dwarf Africans significantly.

Mimulus Relatively new as a bedding plant, now available in a variety of sizes and a wide range of sparkling colours. Very quick to flower from seed so ideal as an emergency filler. Malibu, 6 in. (15 cm), is being superseded by Magic, 6 in. (15 cm), in a wider range of colours, including bicolours, while Calypso, 9 in. (23 cm), has large spotted flowers in a wide range. 'Viva', 12 in. (30 cm), is bright yellow with red spots. Sow late, grow cool, plant in sun or partial shade and do not allow to become too dry. If drought curtails flowering, soak well and clip over lightly.

Nemesia Now enjoying a revival, nemesias come in an enchanting range of mixtures and separate colours, in large- and small-flowered forms. They are at their best in cooler parts of the country. Carnival, 9-12 in. (23-30 cm), is a large-flowered, brightly coloured mixture, Tapestry (Pastel), 9 in. (23 cm) (see p. 46), is smaller flowered with softer colours. 'Blue Bird', 9 in. (23 cm), is a small-flowered, white-eyed blue. The fluffy seed can be difficult to sow evenly. Sow cool and grow on steadily, for nemesias dislike high temperatures. Plant out in partial shade, or full sun

An appealing combination of purple-flowered *Nicotiana* Sensation,
Chlorophytum elatum 'Vittatum' and variegated ivies

with moist soil. Comes into flower early and may burn out by
midsummer, although very colourful in the meantime.

Nicotiana These lovely evening-scented flowers come as tall
border and dwarf bedding cultivars. Sensation, 3 ft (1 m), is a
beautifully scented mix in a wide range of clear colours and
bicolours. *N. affinis*, 3 ft (1 m), is a powerfully scented pure white,
though the flowers may close temporarily in the heat of day.
'Unwins Lime Green', 2 ft (60 cm), is a very strongly coloured
lime-green. Domino, 12 in. (30 cm), is the best short type with
seven colours, some available separately, including picotees. Sow
on the surface and press into compost; relatively quick growing so
grow cool. Look out for whitefly and leafhoppers. Plant in full
sun.

Pelargonium Popular and long-flowering zonal pelargoniums
available in a bewildering range, giving colour all summer. Seed
is expensive but modern cultivars are extraordinarily free
flowering. A few display dramatic leaf zoning. They can be
divided into standards, with relatively small numbers of large
flower heads packed with florets, and floribundas, with a large
number of smaller heads, each with fewer florets; both these
groups reach 12-15 in. (30-38 cm). There are also those
particularly suitable for growing in various containers.

Century, Horizon, Sundance and Gala are all excellent mixtures of the traditional type with many colours available separately, while Pastorale and Torbay Colour Mix are good, less expensive mixtures. There are some lovely separate colours available and I would pick out 'Orange Appeal', a real orange though rather weak, 'Picasso', a purple with an orange eye, the white-eyed pink 'Hollywood Star', the pale pink 'Apple Blossom Orbit' and 'Gala White'. In the floribunda types Multibloom, Avanti and the distinctive Sensation with vast numbers of rather open flower heads, are all impressive mixtures. Again, many individual colours are available, with 'Lucky Break' a good low-cost alternative. Container types include the very compact Video mix, 8 in. (20 cm), for window boxes and small tubs, and for baskets and large tubs the strong-growing 'Breakaway Red' and 'Breakaway Salmon', with spreading habit.

Germinate at 75°F (24°C) if possible until after emergence, then prick out into cells for growing on cooler before potting up individually. Will usually recover from less than ideal treatment after planting. Plant in rich soil in a sunny spot and dead head regularly to promote flowering; this is especially important in the floribunda types.

Petunia Favourite bedders and container plants for their wide range of colours and free-flowering habit, although they can be poor in dull and wet summers. Three main types are available but the distinctions are becoming increasingly blurred and even the seed companies seem confused about where to place some cultivars! Multifloras have large numbers of relatively small flowers; grandifloras branch less strongly, have rather fewer flowers but may be up to 4 in. (10 cm) across; floribundas have large quantities of relatively large flowers. Very few of these are scented, so if scent is a priority an F_2 or open-pollinated mix is most likely to provide it.

The multifloras, 9 in. (23 cm), are good as bedders. The Carpet series is exceptional in its low habit, resistance to grey mould and recovery after rain. It now outclasses the old favourite Resisto series although 'Resisto Rose' is still outstanding in poor summers. The curiously named Plum Pudding is a fine-veined mix. Mirage is the best floribunda, 12 in. (30 cm), and probably the best of all petunias for bedding with its large flowers in generous quantities and its impressive recovery after bad weather. It also features some stunning individual colours. Celebrity runs it close. The grandifloras, 12 in. (30 cm), are not good in poor weather and are best as patio or basket plants where they can benefit from a little shelter. Supercascade is a stunning mix with very large flowers and a slightly trailing habit, 'Supercascade Lilac' ('Birthday Celebration') is an outstanding separate colour. The Supermagic series has darker colours. Hulahoop is a very dramatic white-edged mix while the Daddy series are all strongly veined. Doubles, 12-15 in. (30-38 cm), need even more shelter than the grandifloras although the Duo mix is less fully double and does better in the open. In conservatories Double Delight and the purple and white 'Purple Pirouette' are very impressive.

Sow thinly and uncovered, prick out carefully and grow cool to encourage branching. Prick out those for containers into individual pots, space others well in trays. Look out for aphids. Petunias will tolerate relatively dry conditions, so plant in full sun.

Phlox A unfashionable bedder but much improved in recent years; new cultivars are less straggly and have a better colour range. Of the large-flowered types, Hazy Days, 9 in. (23 cm), has the best range of colours while Palona, 9 in. (23 cm), is more bushy. Of the small-flowered ones, Twinkles, 6 in. (15 cm), is a white-eyed, frilly-edged mixture. Sow in well-drained compost, germinate and grow cool and beware of damping off. Plant in a sunny spot.

Salvia As well as the familiar short scarlet salvias there are two other more elegant types worth growing. Traditional salvias are

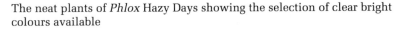

The neat plants of *Phlox* Hazy Days showing the selection of clear bright colours available

also now available in a wider range of colours. Among these, 'Red Riches', 12 in. (30 cm), is a splendid scarlet and with deep green foliage, and 'Blaze of Fire', 12 in. (30 cm), a more economical though rather variable alternative. 'Rambo', 2 ft (60 cm), is taller and more spreading. 'Phoenix Purple', 12 in. (30 cm), is a lovely rich shade while Phoenix Mixed, 12 in. (30 cm), contains purple, white, lilac and two salmon shades as well as scarlet. Pharaoh, 15 in. (38 cm), is an unusual biocoloured mixture. More unusual still is *S. farinacea* 'Victoria', 18 in. (45 cm), with narrow deep blue spikes over grey-green leaves, while *S. coccinea* 'Lady in Red', 18 in. (45 cm), is bushy and less formal in habit than traditional red salvias.

Sow uncovered but ensure high humidity, for without warm, moist conditions germination may be poor. Prick off into individual pots if possible and grow on warm at first, feeding regularly, and harden off carefully. *S. farinacea* and *S. coccinea* are less fussy.

Tagetes Dome-shaped plants with finely cut, scented foliage and vast quantities of small single flowers. Colours are typified by the following: 'Lemon Gem', 'Golden Gem', 'Tangerine Gem' and the rusty red 'Paprika', all 9 in. (23 cm). Starfire is a good mixture. Easy to raise in the same way as French marigolds.

Verbena Increasingly popular plants, slowly overcoming the problems of poor germination and mildew. Most seed-raised plants are much more compact than those raised from cuttings (page 45), all reaching about 9 in. (23 cm). Romance is a sparkling white-eyed mixture but some of the individual colours are especially attractive. 'Blue Lagoon' is deep blue with no eye, 'Showtime Belle' is rich purplish-pink, 'Peaches and Cream' opens coral-pink then fades almost to white. To get the best germination, soak the compost with fungicide the day before sowing, sow thinly and cover with grit or vermiculite. Do not then water until germination. Prick out into cells or individual pots if possible.

Zinnia Very showy plants becoming increasingly popular following hot summers but disappointing in wet seasons. There are two types, tall or bushy with large flowers, and small flowers with a more spreading habit. Belvedere, 12 in. (30 cm), is a mixture which has done well in most summers while Ruffles, 2 ft (60 cm), has especially large flower heads. 'Envy', 2 ft (60 cm) (see p. 31), is an unusual green shade. Of the smaller-flowered types, Persian Carpet, 15 in. (38 cm), is a lovely mix of bicoloured double flowers while 'Orange Star' ('Classic'), 9 in. (23 cm), is a good single orange, 'Ivory', 12 in. (30 cm), a single white.

Sow late, germinate warm but do not overwater. Prick out early into cells or pots and continue to keep on the dry side. Zinnias have a tendency to rot at soil level but cautious watering combined with drenches of a copper fungicide should keep it at bay. Plant out in full sun, water thoroughly, then leave to establish without further watering.

Other summer bedders As well as these, the most popular seed-raised bedding plants for summer, there is a huge range of other attractive summer bedders. Bedding **calceolarias** with their tiny yellow slippers flower all summer; 'Midas', 12 in. (30 cm), is a good cultivar which can be grown cool but may need an occasional dose of sequestered iron. For window boxes and baskets the trailing *Campanula isophylla* is very useful and Stella in both blue and white is ideal, although the seed is small and expensive. Good **heliotropes** are now available from seed and the dwarf 'Mini-Marine', 15 in. (38 cm), has metallic blue foliage and dark blue flowers plus a fine scent; other cultivars are slow to flower and rather straggly.

A number of new **matricarias** (*Tanacetum parthenium*) have appeared recently; 'Butterball', 9 in. (23 cm), is creamy yellow and

Salpiglossis Casino on trial at the Royal Horticultural Society's Gardens at Wisley

Zinnia 'Envy' (see p.29) has flowers of an unusal colour which, if used carefully, can add drama to a bedding scheme

the white 'Snow Crown', 18 in. (45 cm), has tight white flowers with a ring of small petals. In hot, dry situations **mesembryanthemums** always perform well, while **nolanas** are valuable spreaders for beds and containers; 'Bluebird', 6 in. (15 cm), is pale blue with a yellow throat. **Pansies** are best as winter and spring bedders but most will also do well in summer, especially in cool seasons. The Imperial series, 9 in. (23 cm), are bred for summer and come in very distinctive colours such as 'Imperial Silver Princess', a pink-eyed cream, and 'Imperial Gold Princess', a red-eyed yellow. For foliage *Ricinus*, the castor oil plant, is easy to raise and quick growing; 'Impala', 3 ft (1 m), has large, reddish-bronze, sycamore-like foliage. **Rudbeckias** may come in marigold colours but the double-flowered 'Goldilocks' and the rusty-brown 'Rustic Dwarfs' are taller and less squat. The RHS trial at Wisley showed that **salpiglossis** is a fine summer bedder; Casino, 12 in. (30 cm), is especially good outside and can be raised in the same way as petunias.

Tender Perennials from Cuttings

In recent years there has been a revival in the use of those tender perennials which are suitable for growing outside in the summer months, and a growing awareness of the range of plants suitable for this purpose. Abutilons, argyranthemums, gazanias, foliage helichrysums and verbenas are now much more widely seen than even five years ago, old-fashioned favourites have been rediscovered, new ones like scaevolas introduced; many have proved especially useful in containers.

These plants have a number of positive features. Whether their habit is bushy or trailing, many make substantial plants – an attractive feature at a time when there is a trend for seed-raised plants to be increasingly dumpy. They also tend to have a great deal more style than those raised from seed. The majority flower right through the summer, often starting before planting out time and sometimes continuing into December, giving unsurpassed garden value. Most are vigorous and easy to grow, usually thriving in a variety of conditions.

The one drawback is that they must be overwintered in frost-free conditions. With a few exceptions, they are easy to raise from cuttings but they still need frost protection over the winter months. Some can sit on the windowsill indoors, while mature specimens of others will flower in the conservatory right through the winter. But if you only want a few for hanging baskets or tubs, it is best simply to buy fresh plants each spring.

If you intend to replace your plants each spring, then you need no equipment at all; just buy your plants and put them in. You will find that even well established plants in 5 in. (13 cm) pots are excellent value for money. If you decide to overwinter stock, you will need facilities and equipment for taking and rooting cuttings, overwintering plants and growing and hardening them off – in reality much the same as is needed for raising bedding plants from seed. But you will find that if you only intend to overwinter a few, you can get by with a space on a windowsill and an unheated propagator. A thermostatically controlled heated propagator is useful for rooting cuttings, but not essential, depending on which of my suggested regimes you adopt.

PROPAGATION AND OVERWINTERING

These two subjects are best taken together, for the way you overwinter your plants depends on when you propagate. There are three main approaches to this, depending on the facilities at your disposal and the number of plants you want to overwinter. The technique of actually taking the cuttings is the same in each case, but the timing and care vary.

The tips of the shoots make the best cuttings and ideally they should be without flowers; some plants produce flowers on every shoot in which case simply pinch off both flowers and buds. Carefully pinch off the leaves on the lower half of the cutting then trim the stem to just below a leaf joint. Fill a 3½ in. (9 cm) pot with a moistened 50:50 mixture of peat-based cutting or potting compost and grit or perlite for drainage, then insert half a dozen cuttings up to their lowest leaf. Rooting hormones are not necessary.

My first regime will allow you to overwinter adequate stock of the maximum number of different species in the smallest space. This is ideal if your frost-free greenhouse space is limited. Cuttings are taken in late summer in exposed gardens or early autumn in protected areas, depending on where you live. The idea is to leave it as late as possible but still take them before the first frosts. The cuttings are rooted in a heated propagator and once rooted are removed to an unheated propagator or greenhouse at

Tip cuttings. 1 Stem cuttings should be taken from non-flowering shoots. 2 Remove the bottom leaves. 3 Insert several cuttings round the edge of a pot and water them in

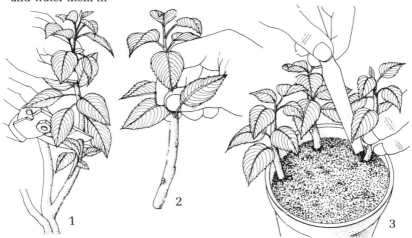

A cool combination of *Nicotiana* 'Nikki Lime' and *Abutilon pictum* 'Thompsonii'

about 45°F (7°C). They spend most of the winter, still in their pots, at a temperature maintained just above freezing, with plenty of ventilation on warm days. The aim is to keep them virtually dormant until spring with the stock of each individual species taking up the space of just one pot and with minimum energy expended on heat. Watering must be very sparing right through the winter.

In spring, there are two ways of continuing depending on the state of the cuttings by March; you can either pot them up into their own individual 3½ in. (9 cm) pots, pinch them and grow them on in the cool, or, if they have become woody and leggy, increase the temperature and the watering, then use the tips to make fresh cuttings.

My second regime requires slightly higher temperatures and allows you to overwinter fewer species in the same space, but by planting-out time you will have far more plants of each. Cuttings are taken in August or early September and after rooting are pinched out and potted into individual 3½ in. (9 cm) pots, using a standard compost. Cuttings are best taken earlier rather than later and the plants moved into 5 in. (13 cm) pots before the winter and kept growing at about 45°F (7°C). During winter, if kept just above freezing, there is an increased danger of root rot and grey mould on the foliage. In the spring the tips of all the side shoots are used as cuttings and the plants kept growing, soon yielding a fresh crop of tips for more cuttings. By planting-out time you will have a small number of large plants in 5 in. (13 cm) pots, although these would benefit from potting on if they are to be planted out, together with a large number of plants in smaller pots.

The alternative is to use windowsills, concentrate on a small number of species and take cuttings in August or September. They can be rooted in an unheated propagator or in a pot covered with a polythene bag; use a windowsill out of direct sun. Pot a couple of rooted cuttings of each species into 3½ in. (9 cm) pots and grow these on the windowsill through the winter. Take more cuttings in spring in the same way and pot these up to give vigorous young plants for setting out.

CARE TO PLANTING TIME

For a while you can manipulate the growing temperature to control the young plants' rate of growth but by late April most will be growing strongly. Many plants dislike being pot-bound and may appreciate potting on if they are filling their pots with roots long before planting time. Feeding is useful to keep plants healthy, but avoid high nitrogen feeds as this will promote sappy, delicate growth. You will find that many will be in flower well before planting out but there is no need to remove the blooms. Do not let plants become too spindly; most respond well to pinching as long as they have good light and plenty of space for side shoots to develop. Keep a watchful eye out for pests; aphids, in particular, can multiply at an alarming rate. As with seed-raised plants, hardening off is vital to ensure that young plants are sufficiently acclimatised when they are set out.

PLANTING OUT

The advice on preparation and planting given for seed-raised plants applies here as well (see p. 14). One important factor that is sometimes overlooked by gardeners used to dealing with seed-raised bedding plants is that many of these tender perennials make very substantial plants and so need much more space in which to develop during the season. Some verbenas can easily make 2 ft (60 cm) across, three times the size of their seed-raised relations, while argyranthemums 3ft (1 m) across and almost as high are not unusual in good soil. Conversely, of course, you need fewer plants to fill a given area.

A to Z of Plants
Raised from Cuttings

A stream of new cultivars and hybrids is appearing in this group of plants for the first time in many years. The names of some are very muddled, one plant may be found under a number of different names while different plants may be found under the same name; verbenas and argyranthemums suffer especially from this problem.

Abutilon There are two groups, one grown mainly for flowers and the other for foliage. Of the large-flowered types 'Golden Fleece', 4ft (1.2 m), with large yellow bells and the orange 'Firebell', 3 ft (1 m), are especially good in tubs; 'Ashford Red', 6 ft (1.8 m), and the white 'Boule de Neige', 4.5 ft (1.2-1.8 m), are more vigorous. *A. pictum* 'Thompsonii' has dark, maple-like leaves mottled in yellow with small orange flowers, while *A. megapotamicum* 'Variegatum' has oval or three-lobed, yellow-splashed leaves and small red and yellow bells. All thrive in rich conditions and full sun and also make good conservatory plants in winter, though susceptible to whitefly.

Argyranthemum A group rapidly increasing in popularity, they are sometimes called marguerites or shrubby chrysanthemums. Many have blue-tinted foliage and they come in an increasing range of flower forms: single, various anemone-centred types and doubles. Colours range from white, through a variety of pinks, to reddish tones, plus yellows and creams. Most flower from before planting out until the first sharp frost.

Of the whites, the blue-green-leaved *A. foeniculaceum*, 2 ft (60 cm), is very floriferous, 'Qinta White', 2 ft (60 cm), is a dark-leaved, anemone-centred form and 'Mrs Sanders', 2 ft (60 cm), is a shaggy double. In pink there is the single 'Gill's Pink', 2 ft (60 cm), the stunning anemone-centred 'Vancouver', 2 ft (60 cm), which fades almost to white, and the rather straggly 'Rollison's Red', 2 ft (60 cm) (see p. 62), starting red and fading to pink. In yellow there is the dwarf *A. maderense*, 18 in. (45 cm), with its rue-coloured foliage, while the floppy 'Jamaica Primrose', 2 ft (60 cm),

Tender perennial argyranthemums are becoming available in a wide range of cultivars. This is 'Vancouver'

Fuchsia 'Autumnale' has attractively tinted foliage

is being superseded by the more compact and very floriferous 'Yellow Star', 18 in. (45 cm).

All are best in rich conditions in sun, either in tubs or beds, and because they make substantial plants and spread well, one is enough for a large tub. Look out for aphids on overwintered plants and leaf miner on mature specimens.

Canna Another group with rather muddled names, cannas have roots like flag irises, broad foliage and flowers in various fiery shades. Most reach 4-5ft (1.2-1.5 m), and are ideal as a focal point or at the back of mixed borders. 'Yellow Humbert' has green foliage and bright yellow flowers, 'Orchid' has pink flowers and green leaves, 'Wyoming' has orange flowers and purple leaves, with 'The President' in deep red with purple leaves. Start the rhizomes into growth in 8-10 in. (20-25 cm) pots in March at 60°F (15°C), harden off and plant out after the last frost. Cannas like a rich soil, plenty of moisture and a sunny spot, and will then increase rapidly. Store the rhizomes frost-free over the winter like dahlias but do not allow them to become too dry.

Dahlia Of the many thousands of dahlias available, the dwarf bedders, 12-18 in. (30-45 cm) and those used in parks, 2-2½ ft (60-75 cm), are the most suitable, although taller cultivars can be used in larger schemes. On the whole, the small and medium cactus, waterlily and decorative forms are the most effective. It would be invidious to make recommendations when so many are available in such a wide range of shades and when most are stocked by just a few nurseries; this indicates how high the general standard is.

There are a few taller, dark-leaved dahlias which are especially worth growing, in particular 'Bishop of Llandaff', 3 ft (1 m), a glowing semi-double scarlet with almost black leaves and 'David Howard', 4 ft (1.2 m), a fully double, fiery orange with bronze foliage. Start the tubers into growth in the warmth in spring, take cuttings of 2-3 in. (5-8 cm) shoots in the propagator, pot on, harden off well before planting. Taller types will need support. Dead head regularly and beware aphids and earwigs and also red spider mite in hot dry summers.

Felicia Invaluable blue-flowered daisies for the sunniest situations, felicias are neat in growth and tougher than many tender perennials. They flower incessantly. 'Santa Anita', 12 in. (30 cm), boasts the largest flowers and also has a yellow variegated form, 'Santa Anita Variegated', 12 in. (30 cm). 'Read's White' is a useful white form but less effective than the blue. Easy to grow, green-leaved types in particular need trimming occasionally to prevent straggliness.

Fuchsia Although fewer gardeners use fuchsias in their bedding than was once the case, more are being used in baskets and window boxes and they really are very effective provided the right cultivar is chosen for the right situation. Some will even thrive on the sunless, north-facing side of a house.

There is a huge range of candidates, both of upright types for bedding and trailing types for baskets, so choose the colours that appeal. I would especially recommend those with coloured foliage, and of the upright ones I suggest *F. magellanica* 'Versicolor' with pale-edged, grey leaves and pink-flushed tips. For baskets 'Autumnale' with its coppery and rusty tints is good, as is 'Golden Swingtime', the yellow-leaved version of the well known red-and-white-flowered cultivar. Another favourite for baskets is 'Golden Marinka', with gold edged leaves and red flowers.

Most fuchsias are best in partial shade although the *triphylla* group which includes 'Thalia' are better able to stand full sun; unfortunately these require a higher winter temperature. Fuchsias appreciate good soil and steady moisture plus regular feeding for container-grown plants. They are better after overwintering as plants rather than as cuttings in pots. Check for whitefly and aphids.

Gazania Although seed-raised gazanias are improving, those

Gazania uniflora grows here in a striking combination with *Tradescantia pallida* 'Purpurea'

raised from cuttings, 12 in. (30 cm), generally have the best foliage, either variegated or silvery white, which ensures they are still attractive on those dull days when the flowers close. Of those with white and silver leaves, 'Cream Beauty' and the orange *G. uniflora* are especially good while the orange-flowered *G. rigens* 'Aureo-Variegata' has strongly yellow-edged leaves. Plant in full sun.

Geranium see **Pelargonium**

Helichrysum Mainly silver-leaved plants which are indispensable in both containers and borders. Most are vigorous with long shoots which insinuate themselves through neighbouring plants, and they look especially good with pastel colours. They can be trained as standards.

There are four main forms of *H. petiolare*. The species itself, 12-18 in. (30-45 cm), is vigorous and has heart-shaped grey leaves, 'Limelight', 12-18 in. (30-45 cm), with yellowish-green foliage is as vigorous, 'Variegatum', 12-18 in. (30-45 cm), with cream-edged leaves is a little less so, while 'Roundabout', 9 in. (23 cm), is compact and variegated. *Plecostachys serpyllifolia* is a small-leaved, bushy, rather similar grey-leaved plant formerly known as *Helichrysum microphyllum*.

An unusual combination of colours is provided by *Heliotropium* 'Chatsworth' and the rust-coloured *Calceolaria* 'Boughton'

Best in sun, partial shade also suits them but they are surprisingly susceptible to drought, especially in containers. *H. petiolare* is hardy in mild areas.

Heliotropium Grown for their vanilla scent as much as their purple or lilac flowers, heliotropes are always admired when well grown. 'Princess Marina', 18 in. (45 cm), is deep purple, 'Chatsworth', 18 in. (45 cm), is paler, 'White Lady', 12 in. (30 cm), is a lilac-tinted white. Plant in full sun, ideal in containers on a sheltered patio. Keep dry in winter.

Impatiens Although most impatiens (busy lizzies) are raised from seed, New Guinea hybrids and some doubles are better from cuttings. The foliage and flower colour of New Guinea hybrids raised from cuttings are superior to seed-raised plants, but they are often sold only in mixed sets or unnamed. Doubles raised from seed will give some singles and a mixture of partial and full doubles; cuttings-raised plants will be good doubles but again are often sold in unnamed mixtures. Best as container plants, grow in sheltered conditions and keep moist. Overwinter as plants rather than cuttings and beware red spider mite both outdoors and in the greenhouse.

Shrubby *Lantana camara* can be trained as a standard plant to grow in a container or form a centrepiece for a bedding scheme

Lantana Unfashionable but delightful plants with a spreading habit and clusters of bright flowers in reds, pinks, yellows, oranges and white but often sold simply by colour rather than by name. Best in full sun, plagued by whitefly in most seasons, so regular treatment will probably be necessary. Rather fragile.

Lotus Delightful, ferny, silver-leaved trailers with parrot's-beak flowers, their spring flowering season means that in summer they are mainly used as foliage plants. *L. berthelotii* has brilliant red flowers in spring on the previous year's growth, 'Kew Form' also flowers in autumn. Full sun and constant moisture encourages the best foliage, drought will cause the needle-like leaves to drop. Overwinter as plants for flowers in the greenhouse in spring.

Osteospermums, like argyranthemums, are becoming very popular with many new cultivars to choose from. This is 'Buttermilk'

Osteospermum Sometimes known as dimorphothecas, osteospermums have daisy flowers in a wide range of colours. They vary in habit and fall into two main groups, the stiffly upright and the flat and ground-hugging, the latter being almost hardy.

'Buttermilk', 2 ft (60 cm), is creamy yellow, 'Whirligig', 2 ft (60 cm), is blue and white with spoon-shaped petals and has a pink version, 'Pink Whirls'; these are upright types. Low-growing 'Cannington Roy', 6 in. (15 cm), is pinkish purple with a white eye, and *O. ecklonis* 'Prostratum', 6 in. (15 cm), is white with a blue eye. There are two upright variegated osteospermums, 'Silver Sparkler', 2 ft (60 cm), with white flowers and white-edged leaves and 'Bodegas Pink', 2 ft (60 cm), with pink flowers and cream-edged leaves.

Osteospermums are best in full sun, with good soil. They are easy to root and overwinter well, but rooted cuttings may continue to grow in even the coolest winter conditions and so need potting up early.

Pelargonium Most zonal and ivy-leaved pelargoniums can be grown outside in the summer months, although the fully double types suffer badly from botrytis. With so many to choose from specific recommendations are unnecessary, but of the zonals the Irenes and the singles with the Highfield prefix are reliable groups, as are the woodier Uniques. All the ivy-leaved types thrive outside but the Cascade series of continental pelargoniums is especially floriferous. Plant them in full sun and although they are drought tolerant they are more prolific, flower longer and keep their foliage better if kept moist but not soggy. They are best overwintered as young plants.

Salvia Most salvias for bedding are raised from seed but better plants of *S. patens*, 18 in. (45 cm), are raised by overwintering. This is an elegant plant with relatively few flowers compared with

Pelargoniums are among the most popular bedding plants, much used in hanging baskets and containers. This is 'Salmon Unique'

seed-raised salvia, but they are much bigger and hooked in shape. The species is rich gentian blue in colour, 'Cambridge Blue' is pale blue, 'Chilcombe' is misty lilac and there is a rare white. This species has tuberous roots and can be overwintered like a dahlia. The best plants are grown by simply replanting the whole root, but cuttings can be taken of the new growth in spring and these will make better plants than seedlings.

Verbena Unlike most seed-raised annual verbenas, those grown as tender perennials are generally spreading in habit and make fine basket and tub plants as well as covering the ground well in borders. There are two groups, dark green with cut leaves and paler green with lobed leaves.

Verbenas are sometimes sold simply by colour which may be red, various purples, lilacs, and pinks plus white and one or two bicolours. 'Lawrence Johnston', 12 in. (30 cm), is a brilliant red, 'Silver Anne', 12 in. (30 cm), a soft pink which is almost hardy, 'Sissinghurst', 9 in. (23 cm), is a cut-leaved cerisey pink, 'Loveliness', 12 in. (30 cm), is deep lilac, 'Carousel , 9 in. (23 cm), is a cut-leaved purple striped with white and 'White Knight', 12 in. (30 cm), is pure white. Full sun suits them best and they are among the easiest of all to grow; some will overwinter outside in mild seasons. Cuttings root very easily, even of old wood, and they usually layer themselves, too.

Other summer bedders from cuttings There are many more tender perennials used as summer bedders, everything from bananas to palms, but there are a few others that you are more likely to come across. The white variegated spider plant, ***Chlorophytum elatum*** 'Vittatum' makes a wonderful bedder but is best planted out as a good-sized plant. The blue-flowered ***Convolvulus sabatius*** with its small, bindweed-like flowers and trailing habit is good in containers, while ***Glechoma hederacea*** 'Variegata' with its small, white-edged foliage trails so determinedly that it simply falls vertically down over the edge of the basket. One cuttings-raised lobelia is worth growing, the semi-trailing ***Lobelia richardii*** with its large pale blue, white-eyed flowers and bronze-tinted foliage. The stiff arching growth of ***Plectranthus coleoides*** 'Variegatus' is very distinctive and very showy in tubs with its white-edged leaves; and **Scaevola**, with flowers like those of perennial lobelias in blue and purple on long trailing shoots, are also fine container plants. Finally, another variegated plant, ***Sedum lineare*** 'Variegatum', with its pale green leaves edged with cream, is proving another good foliage plant for baskets.

Ideas for Summer Bedding

Summer bedding plants are very adaptable. They come in a wide range of colours, flower forms and sizes, so whatever you need for a planned display can be found in the catalogues. It is true that few thrive in full shade but in partial shade and full sun the range is staggering, and choosing superb plants for the traditional combination of red salvia, blue lobelia and white alyssum is as easy as getting away from it altogether and trying something quite different.

BEDDING SCHEMES

Formal bedding schemes provoke strong opinions – some people love them, others will not have them in the garden and even dislike them in parks. But in the right situation, especially in formal gardens, they can be very successful, and in these days of interest in unusual plants a formal bedding scheme featuring an imaginative combination of colourful but slightly unexpected plants can be very successful.

The parks approach, which infiltrated private gardens long ago, was to use a low edging surrounding a slightly taller carpet with dot plants for emphasis; plants raised from seed and from cuttings were mixed. A modern example might feature an edging of bronze-leaved *Lobelia* 'Crystal Palace' with a main planting of *Tagetes* 'Solar Sulphur' Afro-French marigolds with, in a large bed, a clump of *Ricinus communis* 'Impala' added. Segmented circles were also popular and in recent years plantings with curved outlines within a rectangular bed are being used more. Showing off one variety entirely on its own, especially a mixture like *Pelargonium* Sensation or *Impatiens* Super Elfin Pastel, perhaps with silver foliage, can be stunning.

Informal plantings are often more suitable, with beds of a less regular outline planted in less regimental fashion. In fact, the same rules that apply to planting a herbaceous or mixed border can apply to bedding except that you can rely on most summer

Aptly called Tapestry, this mixture of *Nemesia* (see p.25) would look pretty in a bed on its own bedders to flower all summer, so you can largely forget the problem of flowering time.

Perhaps this is the time to sound a warning about mixtures. Most bedders are available in mixtures and are very popular, but they must be used carefully. Planting mixtures of different plants alongside each other is usually a recipe for disastrous clashes; they are best used alone or separated from other mixtures by foliage plants or single colours. But in the same way that planting five different colours of Michaelmas daisy in one clump in a herbaceous border would rarely be successful, mixtures of bedding plants can also disappoint. My advice is always to give them a bed or a corner of their own.

Arranging a bedding scheme like a herbaceous border gives an appropriately informal look. Plants are set in groups of varying informal shapes and although the tallest should generally go at the back of the bed or the centre of island beds, and the planting then grade down to the smallest at the front, this must be a variable rule. Bedding plants are also much more flamboyant than perennials, so you may have to consider using more foliage plants or flowering plants with valuable foliage than you would otherwise – the effect might be just too shocking. Thus coloured-leaved fuchsias, some of the more delicately coloured pelargoniums including scented-leaved types, cannas, abutilons, silver-leaved cinerarias and artemesias can all be invaluable in maintaining a calm tone.

BEDDING WITH PERMANENT PLANTINGS

Leaving spaces in mixed borders for groups of bedding plants allows you an element of change in an otherwise relatively permanent planting. Each summer and spring you can add welcome variation to your borders. Many gardeners are worried by the fact that some bedding plants look out of place in mixed or herbaceous borders. So the plants you choose must not only be of a colour appropriate to nearby shrubs or perennials but must also have a habit and bearing that fit in – otherwise the effect will make you cringe. Fortunately it is usually possible to find exactly the right plant. For example, you may be looking for a fiery orange flower to go at the front of a border alongside the perennial *Heuchera* 'Palace Purple'; a dwarf African marigold might look ridiculous while *Sanvitalia procumbens* would be ideal and could be followed by a dainty viola for spring.

CONTAINERS

Plants specially intended for tubs and hanging baskets are appearing more frequently in garden centres and catalogues. Although the more compact bedders are suitable, plants with a trailing habit are useful to tumble cheerfully over the edge. Plants which tolerate root competition, limited soil space, and the possibility of drying out are invaluable. Watering is usually the problem; if you can rely on containers never being neglected for a scorching weekend, then use mimulus and impatiens; if not, stick to pelargoniums and cineraria. Purpose-made container composts with extra water-holding capacity help the plants withstand drought but watering must be frequent and generous in late summer when temperatures are high and water loss is at its greatest, while roots fill the container and extract moisture at a rapid rate.

Foliage is invaluable in containers as it knits plantings together both in a physical way and by creating allies of neighbouring colours. The silver-leaved *Plecostachys serpyllifolia* will link together pink *Argyranthemum* 'Vancouver', *Lobelia* 'Light Blue Fountain' and perhaps a white multiflora petunia to make a lovely picture.

A colourful combination of argyranthemums, lobelia, fuchsia and bidens

Spring Plants

Compared with the vast array of flowers available for summer from both seed and cuttings, the selection for spring is relatively sparse. Fortunately it does include two groups, pansies and primulas, which provide an exceptionally full range of colours. There is also more scope than in summer for using bulbs with the bedding plants to create a more varied display.

SPRING BEDDING FROM SEED

Almost all spring bedding plants are raised from seed and there are two main methods. Traditionally most were raised entirely out of doors, starting off by sowing the seed in a seed bed in summer. In recent years more plants have been raised under glass and this is partly a response to the increasing cost of F_1 hybrid seed and the relatively small number of seeds supplied in a packet.

RAISING OUT OF DOORS

Virtually no facilities or equipment are required for raising seed out of doors, but the soil should be rich, reasonably well drained and ideally shaded for about half the day; a part of the vegetable plot is often ideal. Plants suitable for raising outside include wallflowers, sweet williams, daisies, forget-me-nots, honesty and the cheaper pansies.

Seed is sown thinly in rows in June or July, just as you would sow hardy annuals or vegetables. If the soil is dry, it pays to water the individual rows from the spout of the watering can immediately before sowing the seed. After germination, the seedlings are thinned carefully, first to 1 in. (2.5 cm) apart, then thinned again, the distance depending on the plant and the cultivar. Place a finger on either side of each seedling to be retained so that it is not disturbed when its neighbour is removed.

The next stage depends largely on the plant concerned, how many seedlings you have and how many you need. Wallflowers

Wall pots filled with pansies and trailing ivy, a simple and pleasing arrangement for winter and spring and sweet williams are best transplanted 6-9 in. (15-23 cm) apart to give them plenty of space to grow on; pansies and daisies can simply be thinned to 4-6 in. (10-15 cm) apart although if you need every seedling these, too, can be transplanted. They will need a thorough watering after thinning or transplanting and will also appreciate a little more sun at this stage. Protect them from slugs and aphids.

RAISING INDOORS

Some seed is too expensive to risk in the open ground and is best raised in a greenhouse or cold frame; this applies especially to pansies, polyanthus and primroses. These are sown in pots in the same way as summer bedding and then stood under the bench in a cold greenhouse or outside in a shaded frame to germinate. Standard peat, coco-fibre or loam-based composts are all suitable but all-peat composts may need additional drainage. They should be pricked out into trays at 35 seedlings to a standard tray, again using a standard compost, then for the best-quality plants they should be moved on individually into 3½ in. (9 cm) pots. If you only need a small number of plants of each variety you could prick them out directly into pots. Propagation trays divided into cells are also useful here. After pricking out they should be grown on in a shady frame. Do not keep them in the warmth of the greenhouse as growth will be leggy.

If you have no greenhouse or frame but still wish to give expensive seed the care it deserves, then sow in pots, stand the pots in a deep box in a shady corner and cover it with shade netting or sacking to keep the seed cool and exclude birds and mice. Prick out into trays and stand them in a cool, partially shaded spot or one shaded from the side rather than overhead. Stand the trays on stones to keep out worms and protect them from slugs.

PLANTING OUT

Plants grown in the open ground should be planted in the autumn, generally about the end of September when the summer bedding is finished, but the exact timing will vary from season to season. Lift the plants carefully, keeping as much soil as possible on the roots. Place them in a box and cover the roots in soil to protect against drying out until replanted. Plant firmly in their flowering place and water in well. Plants raised in trays are generally best

White double daisies, *Bellis perennis*, and wallflowers make an attractive display for a raised, round bed

planted in the autumn, too, so that they have a little time before the winter to settle down. When planting a bed or container with a mixture of bedders and spring bulbs, it is usually impractical to plant the bulbs in the autumn and the bedders in spring. Plant the bedders in autumn and set the bulbs amongst them immediately afterwards.

Pot-grown plants can be planted in the autumn or can be kept through the winter in a cold frame. They should not be over-protected, but covered only in periods of hard frost, gales or downpours. If the plants are cosseted they will grow soft and be easily damaged when they are finally planted out in spring.

Most spring bedders, including pansies and primulas, are best in a rich soil that is not too wet and in full sun; most will also tolerate partial shade but full overhead shade is a less successful situation unless the trees casting the shade come into leaf late. The compost for containers needs to be well drained, especially if planted in the autumn.

Ideas for Spring Bedding

In general, spring bedding plants are suited to a wider range of situations than summer plants. They are less gaudy, less dumpy in their habit and so fit in much better with other spring plants. Like summer plants, their uses can be divided into bedding schemes, plantings in permanent borders and containers.

As well as the traditional bedding scheme of a dwarf edging surrounding a taller carpet and the mixing of wallflowers and bulbs, many spring plants look good as plantings of single colours or mixtures, and in less formal plantings in formal beds. Wallflower 'Primrose Bedder' is lovely edged with pansy 'Joker' or forget-me-not 'Marine'. 'Blood Red' wallflowers can be interplanted with 'White Triumphator' lily-flowered tulips for example, and wallflower 'Harlequin' and pansy 'Ultima' make especially attractive mixed plantings. Sweet williams, being later flowering than most spring plants, are best treated separately.

Most spring plants fit well into mixed borders; only some of the more garish pansies and polyanthus are best kept to themselves. Unfortunately there are no spring plants of a height sufficient to make an impact at the back of the border except foxgloves, but with so few other plants to obscure the view in April and May, plants such as honesty, sweet williams and taller wallflowers can still be very effective.

Tubs, window boxes and hanging baskets, especially in sunny and sheltered spots, are ideal sites for spring plants, for that slight protection will encourage strong growth and early flowering. It pays to keep spring schemes simple – just one variety of pansy, for example, or pink daisies with blue grape hyacinths. Containers provide the ideal site for some of the many pansies in unusual shades which have appeared in recent years, and for primroses and polyanthus in more interesting colours. Many of the primroses in seed catalogues are not hardy enough for the open garden, so have a better chance in a sheltered container.

Red and yellow tulips interplanted with wallflowers in matching colours, and blue forget-me-nots

A to Z of Plants for Spring Bedding

Although there are far fewer spring plants available in catalogues, in some subjects there is an astonishing variety.

Bellis Double daisies come with either neat pompons or larger, shaggier flowers. The colours are restricted to reds, pinks and white. Spring Star, 4-6 in. (10-15 cm), is a large-flowered, pompon mix which includes an unusual blood-red shade; Pomponette, 4-6 in. (10-15 cm), has smaller pompon flowers in three shades while Goliath, 6-8 in. (15-20 cm), has shaggy flowers up to 3 in. (8 cm) across. Best sown in the open and transplanted, these daisies are lovely window box plants, and good edging for small beds.

Forget-me-not (*Myosotis*) This spring favourite is easy to raise and its airy habit makes it an ideal contrast with other plants. There are tall and some rather dumpy forms. 'Marine', 6 in. (15 cm), is deep blue, 'Ultramarine', 10 in. (25 cm), is the best all round variety, while 'Blue Bouquet', 15 in. (38 cm), is good in larger borders. There are also those with pink and white flowers but these are generally less successful. Raise in the open ground or in boxes; in dry seasons their display may be curtailed by mildew.

Foxglove (*Digitalis*) Foxgloves may last for several years but flower best in the second year and move well in autumn. Excelsior, 5 ft (1.5 m), is a wonderful tall mixture, Foxy, 3 ft (1 m), is more compact. Both have flowers all around the stem. For bedding, raise outside and transplant with plenty of soil on the roots.

Honesty (*Lunaria annua*) Biennials which are often left to self-sow, they make impressive bedders and being taller than wallflowers are especially valuable. 'Munstead Purple', 3 ft (1 m), is rich purple while 'Alba', 3 ft (1 m), is pure white. Raise outside, taking especial care to keep the soil on the roots when transplanting.

Excelsior foxgloves bring colour to a mixed border when most of the plants are still only in leaf

Pansy and viola (*Viola*) The most popular spring bedders, now available in an astonishing range of colours. Some are known as winter-flowering and will flower in the autumn, in mild spells in winter and swing into their stride early in spring; others are more genuinely spring flowering. Violas are smaller flowered, more dainty and spring flowering.

The best winter-flowering mixture is Ultima in 27 shades although Universal is still popular; Ultima Pastel Mix includes only the pale shades and is very pretty. Many of the colours in the Ultima and Universal mixtures are available separately. Of the spring pansies Turbo and Majestic Giants are good while Spring Ovation is a more economical mix. 'Jolly Joker' is a cheeky blue and white, 'Delft' is cream and blue, 'Padparadja' is orange and Love Duet is cream or white with a raspberry blotch. The catalogues list many other delightful and unusual colours. In violas Bambini is a gold eyed mixture while Princess is a lovely mixture of blue, yellow, cream and a purple/white bicolour.

Sow indoors and grow on in trays or pots. Keep cool and on the dry side, planting out in winter or spring. Ideal for bedding and especially good in window boxes and in hanging baskets.

Polyanthus (*Primula*) An old favourite for spring, there are those with large flowers and bright colours as well as ones in more subtle and unusual shades. Some have been developed as pot plants and may perform poorly in the open garden.

Crescendo, 9 in. (23 cm), is a large-flowered mixture in seven yellow-eyed shades, Rainbow, 9 in. (23 cm), in eight eyed shades has smaller flowers but more of them and is usually more effective. These can be planted in the autumn with confidence. The Pacific Giants, 12 in. (30 cm), are less hardy and are best set out in spring. The Barnhaven series, 9 in. (23 cm), come in some wonderful pastel shades and rich eyeless colours, are perfectly hardy but are now difficult to obtain.

Polyanthus are best raised in a cold greenhouse or frame but should be kept cool as high temperatures can inhibit germination. Ensure the seed compost is well drained, do not cover the seed with compost but keep humid with glass or clingfilm. Sieve a little compost over the seed as soon as it has germinated to anchor the seedlings.

Primrose (*Primula*) Most primroses in the catalogues are intended to be grown as pot plants and although some may be grown successfully in containers in sheltered spots, few thrive in the open garden. As well as the usual bright colours, there are dainty bicolours and those with dark leaves.

The Wanda Hybrids have attractive foliage and flowers in a range of subtle, old-fashioned colours

The pick of the bedding primroses are undoubtedly the Wanda Hybrids, 4-6 in. (10-15 cm) which are vigorous, very hardy and come in a range of seven colours, all with rich green or bronze-tinted leaves. Husky, 6 in. (15 cm), is a good, brightly coloured, green-leaved mix. The Juliana Hybrids, 4-6 in. (10-15 cm), in a wide range of dainty bicolours, are a little less tough. Raise them in the same way as polyanthus.

Stocks (*Matthiola*) Wonderfully scented plants in delightful soft shades, ideal for patio containers. Two types feature as spring bedders, Brompton stocks and East Lothian stocks. Brompton stocks reach about 18 in. (45 cm), and can be selected for doubleness and flower in May and June. East Lothian stocks reach 9-12 in. (23-30 cm), flower in June and July, but are not selectable for doubles.

Selectable Mixed is the only Brompton mixture which is selectable for doubleness; the doubles have light green leaves and

Massed Brompton stocks with an edging of ivy

these should be grown on for the best plants. Legacy is the best East Lothian type and you should expect 80 per cent doubles. The colours in both mixtures are shades of red, pink, purple, lilac and white.

Both types are best sown in the greenhouse in June or July and pricked out into 3½ in. (9 cm) pots for overwintering in a cold frame before planting out in mid March. Watch for grey mould on the plants during the winter.

Sweet william (*Dianthus*) Of all the dianthus only sweet william are treated as spring bedders. They flower later than most, which means they do not combine well with other spring plants, and they also disrupt the planting of the summer bedding. Auricula Eyed, 18 in. (45 cm), comes in red and pink shades, each with a white eye, Monarch, 18 in. (45 cm), in rich and pastel shades, while Indian Carpet, 9-12 in. (23-30 cm), is a good dwarfer mixture; 'Crimson Velvet', 18 in. (45 cm), is a fine blood-red shade. Sow outside and transplant with plenty of soil on the roots. When grown for cutting, the plants can be left in place for a second year.

Viola see **Pansy**

Wallflowers (*Cheiranthus* and *Erysimum*) Wallflowers are much better raised at home than bought from markets or garden centres where they are usually stood in buckets of water for days while the roots rot; they are very easy and you will be able to grow the separate colours rarely found on sale as plants. They come in three types, taller ones at about 18 in. (45 cm), dwarf ones at 10-12 in. (25-30 cm), and Siberian wallflowers, 9 in. (23 cm), which are a little later flowering and mound forming rather than upright and bushy.

Of the taller ones, Harlequin is a fine mixture and there are some lovely separate colours such as 'Blood Red', the orangey-red 'Fire King', 'Purple Gem' and the bright yellow 'Cloth of Gold'. Bedder is the best of the shorter growing mixtures with separate colours available in gold, orange, primrose and scarlet. Pastel Shades, 12 in. (30 cm), includes many unusual colours not found in most mixtures. 'Orange Bedder' is a brilliant orange Siberian type.

Sow outside from May to July; leave it late in windy areas or your plants will be too big to remain stable after planting out. Wallflowers are susceptible to clubroot so incorporate them into the brassica rotation on the vegetable plot. Do not try to raise them in pots.

'Little Darling' (see p.19) has unusual open-throated flowers. Like other antirrhinums it may suffer from rust

61

Pests and Diseases

Early in the life of spring and summer bedding plants, disease can be prevented by using clean pots and trays, fresh composts (never garden soil) and water direct from the mains, not from a water butt. Preventative treatment with a copper fungicide also helps. Once through the early stages, there is generally no need to spray but checks should be made regularly and any problem dealt with promptly to prevent its spread. Good hygiene, careful watering and drenching with a copper fungicide will help prevent damping off, when seedlings collapse in the pots or trays, and blackleg. Good air flow in frames and greenhouses and regular removal of dead leaves and flowers will help prevent botrytis, but carbendazim spray will cure it. Aphids can be a problem; the specific aphid killer pirimicarb harms few other insects. Powdery mildew can be very destructive in hot seasons on verbenas and violas; propiconazole will deal with it effectively and with rust on antirrhinums. Derris will kill or at least restrict red spider mite and is good against small caterpillars.

Matricaria 'Snow Dwarf' used as an edging plant for a bed of *Argyranthemum* 'Rollison's Red' (see p.37)

Buying Plants and Seeds

For gardeners who do not wish to raise their own plants there are two ways of obtaining them. Many of the mail order seed companies sell seedlings or young plants and while these can be relatively expensive compared with seed, they allow you to bypass the germination stage which some gardeners find the most difficult. The plants sold in this way are not restricted to seed-raised plants, and tender perennials are also offered

Of course, bedding plants are also sold in garden centres, markets and even by the side of the road. The quality varies enormously. Beware of plants which are straggly, have yellow or pale green foliage, are very small, have lots of root emerging from the base of the pot or tray, or are affected by pests or diseases. Do not buy plants which are displayed without protection early in the season. Plants in pots or large cells are more expensive than those sold in strips or trays but are often of better quality and will usually transplant more successfully.

SEED SUPPLIERS

Each of the following mail order companies lists a good range of seeds of bedding plants and most also list seedlings and young plants.

D T Brown, Station Road, Poulton-le-Fylde, Blackpool, FY6 7HX

Chiltern Seeds, Bortree Stile, Ulverston, Cumbria, LA12 7PB

Dobies Seeds, Broomhill Way, Torquay, TQ2 7QW

E W King & Co, Monks Farm, Pantlings Lane, Coggeshall Road, Kelvedon, Essex, CO5 9PG

Marshalls Seeds, Regal Road, Wisbech, PE13 2RF

Mr Fothergill's Seeds, Gazeley Road, Kentford, Newmarket, CB8 7QB

Suttons Seeds, Hele Road, Torquay, TQ2 7QJ

Thompson and Morgan Seeds, London Road, Ipswich, IP2 0BA

Unwins Seeds, Histon, Cambridge, CB4 4ZZ

Index

Page numbers in *italic* type indicate illustrations